Jerome Roams From Home

by Patricia Maness

For information regarding publication write to
Bluewater Publications at
BWPublications.com.

Library of Congress Control Number: 2020907025
Hardback - Jerome Roams from Home & Jerome Roams Back Home Flip Book: 978-1-949711-58-5
Softback - Jerome Roams From Home & Jerome Returns Back Home Flip Book: 978-1-949711-69-1
Ebook - Jerome Roams from Home: 978-1-949711-59-2
Ebook – Jerome Roams Back Home: 978-1-949711-60-8

Special thanks:
Angela Hardgrave -Interior Layout Design
Angela Broyles -Managing Editor

jerome roams from home!

written and illustrated

by patricia maness

to Christy Jo Jordan
and her C3 students
thank you for a special year!

~2010~

Well, it's a long story
cut short ~
　　but it matters!

So, hold on ~

　　and enjoy the ride!

It's worth it ~
　　I promise!

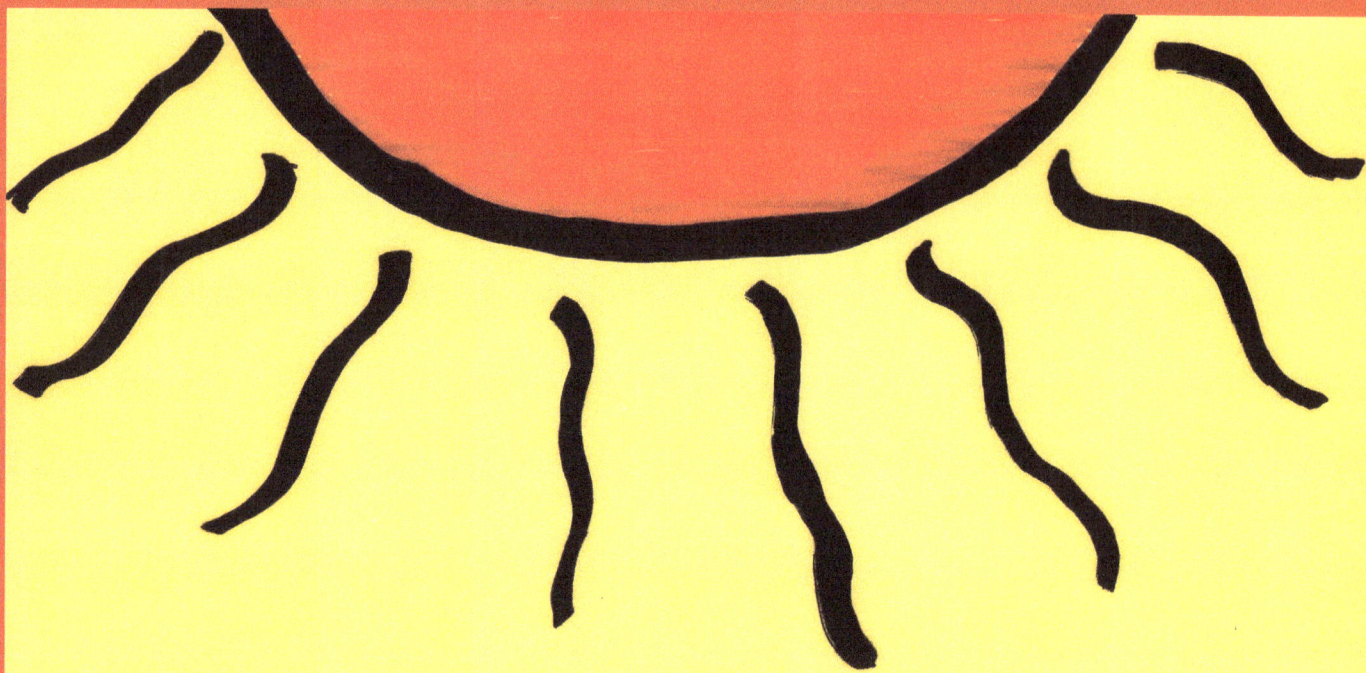

The day was a
beautiful day~

A hooray kind of day
I'd say !

The sun rose slowly
behind the trees~
With all things happy~
even the bees!

The flowers were smiling ~
because today
was the day ~

It was time for him to get moving on ~

Because if he waited ~ the sun would be gone.

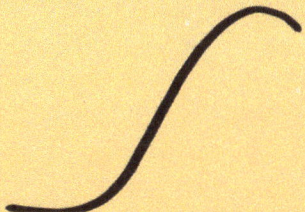

He saw flowers and trees
even birds and bees~

The rhythm
    of the road
was like music
        being made ~

Jerome listened closely~
He heard notes being played!

That it was getting lighter
and brighter
as could be!

Jerome couldn't
believe ~
What he saw
with his eyes!
SUNFLOWERS!
EVERYWHERE!
BRIGHT AND TALL!
He couldn't say
anything ~
Anything at all!

It WAS a beautiful day!

A GRAND hooray

Kind of day!

And Jerome quietly
thought,

"I'm glad, so glad, I
roamed from
home!"

Well, as the long story cut short ends ~

it still matters!
Always enjoy the ride!
Keep your eyes

wide open!
It'll always be worth it~

~ I promise! ~

the
end

It's so fun to roam
but indeed it's true ~
There's nowhere like home
Jerome thinks as much too!

HOME
SWEET
HOME

And as Jerome's journey has come to an end ‿
He's so thankful to have met many a friend!

Remember the lessons along the way ~
'Cause those are important
I'm happy to say!

With eyes wide open and using his ears Jerome saw + heard all there was to see and hear!

ENJOY THE RIDE

Fun Times

Happy Thoughts

No Regrets

Good Times

So, remember the fun times
and forget the bad ⌣
Because they made you happy
and not at all sad!

But then you just think
regrets are so few
You think of the good times
with those that you knew!

I'm so glad
I......

There's beauty all around us
we see it every day ~
Sometimes we take for granted
all the things
that come our way!

As Jerome roamed home
he thought happy thoughts~
About all that he saw
and heard, that's a lot!

TO HOME

There will always be sunrises
and always sunsets~
No two are alike
and that's good as it gets!

Jerome saw the sunrise

and he saw the sunset.

Such beautiful sights

that he couldn't forget!

And as the day
   had started to fade ~
Jerome was sure
   he saw a mermaid!

Amongst the palm trees
the sea oats swayed
And out in the water
the dolphins played!

He saw lots of crabs
and sandpipers too ⌣
Sand castles were built
on the shore by "who knew"?

There were starfish and driftwood
sand dollars as well ~
Some turtles and seagulls
and even some shells!

And look what was there
it was well within reach,
Jerome had roamed on
a most beautiful beach!

He saw and heard oceans
with waves that they made.
They crashed on the sand
but he wasn't afraid!

What happened next
was not a surprise ~
Jerome heard and saw
with his ears and his eyes!

The happy trip along the way
will keep you on your toes~
You'll see so many
different things
and that's just how it goes!

Sometimes it's hard
to leave somewhere
and even though it's sad~
The things you see
along the way
back home will make you glad!

So goodbye sunflowers
I'm ready to roam ~
It's time for me
   to get myself home!

Well, the long story
cut short
        has come to an end ~
for Jerome the Motorhome.
    as he roams home again!
So, I say to you
        without further delay ~
Here we go again
        Jerome's on his way!

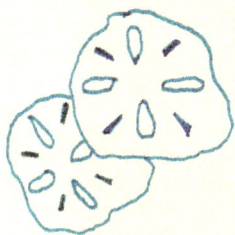

To my husband, Carl,
The love of my life!
Thank you for always
enjoying the ride with me!
And to BEN! Jerome's biggest fan!

Jerome Roams Back Home

written and illustrated by Patricia Maness

For information regarding publication write to
Bluewater Publications at
BWPublications.com.

Library of Congress Control Number: 2020907025
Hardback - Jerome Roams from Home & Jerome Roams Back Home Flip Book: 978-1-949711-58-5
Softback - Jerome Roams From Home & Jerome Returns Back Home Flip Book: 978-1-949711-69-1
Ebook - Jerome Roams from Home: 978-1-949711-59-2
Ebook – Jerome Roams Back Home: 978-1-949711-60-8

Special thanks:
Angela Hardgrave -Interior Layout Design
Angela Broyles -Managing Editor

Jerome Roams Back Home

by Patricia Maness

the
end!